I0568269

Shipping Container Homes

A Guide to Planning, Designing, and Building a Container Home

Mitchell Mills

Table of Contents

Introduction

In the world of modern architecture, you may come across the word "cargotecture." This is a word created to describe the increasingly popular sub-form of architecture where shipping containers are used to create houses. The "cargo" prefix comes from a shipping container's primary use as a means of cargo transportation. If you haven't seen a modified shipping container before, you might be uninterested with this idea. After all, the containers are big and rectangular shaped, so how can living in one be comfortable, much less stylish? Well, there is a lot more that goes into the planning and processing than you might think.

It was a concept that had been circling people's minds for some years. The idea of having smaller housing has been around since the 70s, with several fiction authors writing novels about tiny houses, usually in the woods. Although interest would pique at the notion, this was also around the time when a working-class family on a modest income could purchase a 1,700 square foot rancher home. Certainly, miniature houses were a novel idea, but what was the point when a comfortable, regular-sized house was within the budget?

As the years passed, the housing market faced a shift. Building contractors upped the size of an average home. Ranches went out of fashion. Not only would houses be two floors or more, but the square footage also went up to an average of 2,400. Of course, with these changes came an increase in price. But there was also a lack of smaller family homes being built. It seemed to be that the choices were apartments, condominiums, or oversized suburban houses. Ironically, this went in complete opposition to the sizes of families at the time, which were going down.

So, faced with a lot of big houses with no one to buy them, the forward-thinking architects and contractors began brainstorming for solutions. One offshoot of this was the movement in micro-housing. But there had to be another way, a cheaper way, to create a wide range of small, affordable houses. Enter the shipping container. Shipping containers, or "intermodal freight containers," to be precise, are the large steel boxes used to transport all types of cargo, whether that be over land or overseas. Up to 40 ft in length and rectangular in shape, these containers reach 2.6m—or 8ft 6in—in height. Structurally, they are very sound, durable, and made to withstand severe weather conditions.

More containers enter the U.S. than leave, so there is a high percentage of containers that become unused. The reason for this comes from North America's reliance on importing goods, rather than exporting. Most products come from Asia, more specifically from Indonesia and China, but also from various

European countries. When cargo freighters come into North American ports, they are unloaded with imported products, and then reloaded with products to be sent back. But, due to the dependence on importing, the product being sent back out is only half as much as what came in.

So, the cargo freighter ships are being sent off full of empty containers and being paid to do so. Companies learned quickly that they would actually save money by just buying new containers, rather than paying out to have the empty containers sent back. Hence, the empty containers were taken out of circulation. Rather than let them rust away or waste the considerable energy it takes to melt them down into recyclable steel, the government, alongside various economic groups, set about finding ways to repurpose them.

The first written record of a shipping container being used for housing was in 1987. A patent was filed, with the purpose of being a "Method for converting one or more steel shipping containers into a habitable building at a building site and the product thereof." It took two years, but on August 8th, 1989, patent 4854094 was granted. Though the man who filed for the patent was likely not aware that he would start a trend in thirty years' time, he nevertheless laid the groundwork for everyone who came after.

However, it is unlikely that the concept of creating a living space out of a shipping container sprung fully formed from his head. Before we ever had the container, we had boxcars. Still in use on trains to this day, a boxcar is nearly identical to the modern intermodal freight container, except it is relegated to use on trains. Boxcars had been the residence of the travelling homeless since their creation. It was brought into a slightly more positive light due to the 1924 children's book, *The Boxcar Children*, in which a family of orphans took up residence in an abandoned boxcar. The Great Depression of the 1930s saw a distressing increase in homeless populations, and living out of boxcar trains became all the more popular.

Two years before the patent was filed, in 1985, a science fiction movie titled *Space Rage* made use of shipping containers as background props, styling them as the base architecture on a prison planet. Between that visual and the knowledge of boxcars as living space, the idea likely took root.

After that, the idea of turning shipping containers into homes in the mainstream consciousness came from a surprising source: the U.S. Army. During the Gulf War, the army was looking for quick ways to transport goods. The highly durable shipping containers became an easy way to go about this. However, and almost by accident, the army began using said shipping containers for emergency shelters in moments of high crisis. Quickly after that, they discovered the containers also served a purpose as a safe house for prisoners. By drilling holes for ventilation and lining the walls with sandbags, they created a steady shelter against the threat of an oncoming RPG missile.

The use of shipping containers as a habitable space was further explored and given serious weight in 1994. Author Stewart Brand decided that, while writing his book *How Buildings Learn*, he was going to convert a shipping container into an office space. He did so successfully, and wrote the entire book inside that same office. Within the pages, he outlined the process of how he went about it. When the book was published, more heads were turned in that direction.

The steadily growing interest in shipping container homes hit a particular high after the 2008 financial crisis, a growth that is still ongoing today. Perhaps the most notable thing about shipping container homes is that they go hand in hand with the phrase, "affordable housing." The economy suffered in all areas from the crisis, but where it hit North Americans the hardest was the housing market. As the prices trended higher and higher, the younger generations began looking for new ideas and ways to live affordably in the changing climate. It took a few years to get off the ground, but by 2013, the shipping container home had entered the public social consciousness. They appeared on news specials, television shows, and documentaries.

So that leads us to where we are now. Are you interested in moving your life into a shipping container? There's so much more information than the little history lesson above. Everything you need to know about your future in a shipping container is within these pages, and by the time you have finished, you'll be ready to start planning your future home.

Chapter One: Container Home Features

The charm of shipping container homes lies in their customizable features. Working with a limited square footage means most of the common home features will have to be modified to suit the container home. Dimensions will be reduced, and shapes will be modified to embrace the structure of the container home itself and/or the surroundings. Here are some features that have already proven viable for shipping container homes:

1. **Terraces or pergolas**—made from a spare container with the left and right walls stripped off.

2. **External connecting decks**—a separate assembly of your choice (wood, brick, stone, concrete, etc...)

3. **Window boxes**—attached to the steel framing of the window.

4. **Glass balustrades**—an alternative for terraces, the glass can be held in place by mounted spigots and supported by the terrace's steel pillars.

5. **Skylights**—this can range from a 2x2ft glass roof in a single-container home, or the entire length of the third container with both walls stripped off and then situated in-between two containers that form the

extended sides of the house. Skylights can help reduce electricity costs in the long run because they let in natural light and heat.

6. **Sliding glass doors**—additional functions: reinforces wall and roof supports with steel framing, plus entry point for natural light.

7. **Floor to ceiling shelving systems**—columns of shelves can double as roof support and room division, especially when placed at the center of the container.

8. **High windows**—don't only illuminate the room, but also promote proper ventilation.

9. **Container pools**—this is an extravagant feature that's interesting, to say the least. A spare container with its roof removed can be converted into a traditional pool (the ground is excavated, and the container is lowered in place; tiles are usually laid along the edges of the container pool), or an elevated pool (the container pool sits on the ground, just like the container house, and there will be a ladder and a sitting ledge at the edge of the container).

Utilities

In addition to structural features, you might consider adding features that will help minimize costs for utilities. Several examples above which allow natural light into the house also fall into the utility territory.

The following are features that owners of converted container homes should consider having. Having an unconventional home means that repairs may also be unconventional. The methods of assembly for electric lines, water pipes, septic systems, and heating, for example, are likely to be different from other familiar systems in traditional houses. Hence, there will be a greater payoff if you invest in utility features during the early construction process.

1. **Water tanks**—rainwater collected from the roof can be converted for drinking, or simply for washing.

2. **Solar panels**—they are usually laid on the roof, but may also be assembled on the ground, facing whichever direction will maximize sunlight exposure. Electricity will be stored in batteries. The energy produced is usually enough to power small, basic home appliances.

3. **Air conditioning**—consider the chances of mounting air conditioning units when evaluating the integrity of the walls.

4. **Wood burners**—this saves electricity, but access to firewood will be required. The important points to consider will be the exhaust system and compliance to fire safety codes.

5. **Grills**—installing grills outside windows and doors promotes ventilation, natural lighting, and home security.

6. **Interior insulation**—padding the walls with insulation from the inside, without touching the corrugated walls, will preserve structural integrity in addition to regulating interior temperature.

7. **Satellite dish or antenna mounts**—this is a necessity if the house is in a remote location. This is for cable, telephone, and Internet connections.

8. **Single-sinks**—whether for a bathroom or the kitchen, a single-sink will be space-efficient.

9. **Showers**—for container homes with limited floor space, go for a shower stall instead of a tub.

10. **Lofts**—a cozy feature for single-container homes, a loft is best installed for a 45 ft high-cube container because 9 ½ ft of roof height will leave more room for a loft (which can serve as the sleeping area) and the space beneath it can be utilized for storage or a low-

ceiling living area. The latter is especially possible if the foundation is a crawl space. This means the floor area can be lowered to the ground.

11. **Cooling roof coating**—a must-have for container houses in tropical climates. The low roof will make the entire house prone to humidity and heat. A cool roof coating can at least help deflect UV rays and heat.

The great thing about these features is that if they do not make it to the first construction plans because of budget constraints, they can still be installed at a later date.

Chapter Two: Benefits to Owning a Shipping Container Home

Living in a home constructed from recycled shipping containers has plenty of advantages, and more and more people are beginning to understand this and take action. You will appreciate these advantages first-hand and see them for yourself if you are lucky enough to have created your own and/or live in one. When it comes to building your own home, used containers are versatile, sturdy, modular, and just all-around winners, being much cheaper than traditional construction for timber-framed houses and brick and mortar structures.

Pros

1. Accessibility

When comparing the price of traditional building materials and steel containers, steel containers are cheaper. This is particularly true when you consider the increasing cost of lumber. No house can be constructed without some level of expense, but this will minimize the house's cost in so many ways.

2. Incredible space

Being rectangular in shape, a room can be created from containers easily. Further, containers can come in various sizes, allowing you to be creative and design unique shapes for your house. You can get a 20 by 40 container for your main room and get other sizes for the rest. Since these containers can be bundled together, you can maximize the efficiency of your space.

3. Time-saving

It takes time to construct a traditional building. Prefabricated structures such as containers can easily become a functional office if you suddenly need an office space. This saves the lag inherent to the house-building process. That simple, metal container can quickly become an elegant room. The average time to transport and prepare a shipping container is about two months. This includes the time from the initial purchase to the final touches of personalization required to create a comfortable home or office environment. Furthermore, many companies specialize in fitting containers for a faster build time. It is also possible, for those who want a more hands-on approach, to fully complete the fit in person when the container is shipped and located.

4. Affordable to build

The average cost of this sort of home or office is very affordable. It is cheaper to purchase a container and turn it into a secure and comfortable home than to buy a normal property in a cheap town area. A used container can currently be picked up for about US$1,500. This is the base cost for 305sq feet of floor space. When you compare it to the expense of more conventional building forms, it's a pretty good deal!

5. Environmentally Friendly

So how green can shipping containers be? Essentially, they can be as green as you would like them to be.

Think of your home more like an "eco-pod" if you want to go down an environmentally friendly path. By placing a few solar panels on the roof, you could generate your own electricity. If you're close to a river or a quick-flowing stream, you can use hydroelectric power. A "Green/Living Roof" can also be added to the top of your containers to drastically reduce heating and cooling costs.

6. Weatherproof

Consider the fact that shipping containers are built to travel hundreds of thousands of miles on open-top, trans-oceanic cargo vessels; they are designed to endure the most unforgiving environmental conditions and are constructed to have a minimum work life of 20 years. After that, these containers have an almost endless lifespan in a fixed location – if cared for correctly. They are made from prefabricated steel, making them strong, rigid, and very durable. This makes them especially well-suited for hurricane hotspots and earthquake zones. Shipping containers can withstand up to 175mp/h (281km/h) wind speeds when anchored to pylons, which is easy to do.

7. Excellent flexibility

Once the container has been purchased, the internal configuration and most essential features can be customized. It typically helps to look at various floor plans and floor sizes to understand what is available and create a layout to meet your particular needs. The traditional 20-foot container is an excellent choice to turn into a house since it is simpler to navigate and is better suited for combining with other units. The 40ft model is a choice for those looking for more interior space and provides access to almost 300 sq-ft. Also, the wider containers provide more versatility in separating internal space into different areas.

The boom in shipping container homes has been entirely justifiable in the last few years, and it is no wonder why so many individuals turn to these containers to create their own dream homes. With the right internal floor plans, a comfortable and practical space can be created with everything you need to relax in style.

Although it might seem like there would be many difficulties in turning a container into a home, the whole process is usually straightforward. Obviously, the more basic the design, the easier and more cost-effective the build will be.

Cons

1. Potential Issues with Longevity

Since they have no firm ground floors, the containers are theoretically problematic as an alternative living space. There are of course steps that can be taken to minimize these concerns, such as using a solid foundation and installing quality flooring.

It is undeniable that rust and other environmental damage can deteriorate containers made of metal. For this reason, shipping container homes may need a little extra maintenance compared to their traditional counterparts.

2. Tropical Countries Might Pose a Problem

Heat is absorbed more readily because the material is metal. Containers might not be the best choice if you live in a tropical climate. These locations are not always a practical place for construction because of the high cooling costs involved.

3. They Don't Work Everywhere

Before buying a shipping container home, there are three essential items to remember:

1. **Zoning**—Sadly, in some areas, container homes won't be allowed due to local government regulations. So, be sure to check the rules in the area you wish to build!

2. **Skill**—this might not be a good choice for you if you do not have a knack for renovation. The building will require insulation, walls, plumbing, electrical connections, etc. You know, the home's usual fittings. Fortunately, professionals can be hired to do this work, but obviously additional costs will be involved – particularly if they aren't used to working with containers as a building material.

3. **Significant others**—the notion of transforming shipping containers into houses is a little out-there, to

be honest. While they are becoming more and more popular, it is a common occurrence for people to have a hard time convincing their loved ones to make the move!

Chapter Three: Planning and Designing

So, when it comes to interior design in a shipping container, odds are your choices will be very limited, right? Well, that's not entirely the case. While it is true that a single shipping container does not leave a lot of room for wild designs, that does not mean that you have no interesting options. Think of any apartment on the smaller side. What are the important things it has? It has a bedroom, a bathroom, and a kitchen. Spaces for living and dining are malleable and optional. You could choose to have laundry utilities installed in your shipping container, but you could just as easily decide to use a coin laundromat.

When you think of an open concept kitchen and dining room, consider how they could be translated to the inside of your shipping container. The flow from one to the next is relatively easy. The table and chairs that you would use in a dining room can be replaced with armchairs and a coffee table, combining two functions into one. This has become increasingly popular in interior decoration since the television became a staple in everyone's homes.

An open concept can also be used in the bedroom, giving it a similar look and style to a studio apartment. For a person living by themselves, this is an ideal option for maximizing space.

You don't want to have plain steel floors. All contractors will add new ones when preparing the container, so you can go with whatever you want, though it is a recommendation to stay away from carpets. Not only have they gone completely out of fashion, but it's unwieldy to have to cart a big vacuum around your little shipping container. Keeping the floors wooden, tiled, or mock wood makes it easier for you to clean.

You can note in the above design that they have a dining room/kitchen combined with their living area. What this will come down to is your own style of eating. If you can't stand the thought of eating on the sofa, then you should likely opt for a dining table instead. Consider, too, that a popular trend in kitchen design is to have bar stools at your counter, such as in the design above. This is another good substitute in place of a table.

The bathroom in the above design has a standing shower. With your shipping container home, unless you are using multiple containers for more space, you are almost guaranteed to need a standing shower instead of a bathtub. Though, this is not to say that a tub is completely out of the question. If you decide to put a quarter's worth of space into your container's bathroom, that's entirely your decision. But for a standing shower, the above design uses one with a curved wall. Whether this actually saves space in opposition to a square shower is up for debate, but it does certainly keep it nicely in one corner. Bathrooms are one of those types of spaces that can be kept small without sacrificing any style or function, if designed correctly. Of course, you can also simply add another container to the design to instantly double the space you have to work with!

You will also notice that this design has an entire little room cut aside to act as an entryway. Perhaps you think this is a brilliant use or perhaps you think it is a waste of space. The cubby to hold shoes is certainly cute and cuts down on the closet space needed, but you may wonder how many shoes a person or couple could need. This entry room could be removed and all you would need by the door is a welcome mat and a shoe rack.

One thing many people don't take into consideration when looking at renting apartments is the wall décor. When you are renting, there are rules and regulations against using nails to put things on the walls. Not everything can be supported by sticky tacks, such as large photo frames or paintings. When you build your shipping container home, it is yours to decorate any way you please. This also means you can paint the walls any color you like.

Roofs and Heights

It's been mentioned before that many purchasers of shipping containers choose to invest in a roof. This could be a roof added atop the already existing structure, but you could also choose to cut out the top of the container. By doing this, you could add a little more height and open up room for options; So-called, "High Cube," shipping containers will give you an extra foot of height, with a cut-off ceiling adding even more, even leaving you open to the potential of a loft.

Due to logistics, lofts are usually relegated to micro-housing that is small but tall in comparison. However, with a slightly raised roof, it is possible for you to add a little space big enough for you to put a bed. Lofts are very stylish and seem to be a "love it" or "hate it" addition. It means that the sleeping area won't be tall enough to stand up in, and the area beneath will be much lower and could be too low for a tall person to stand in. Thus, that space might not be as comfortable when used as the kitchen or bathroom, or even the living room; it would, instead, be best relegated to something like a reading nook. But then, not everyone needs something so quirky. Still, if you can get the height, it is certainly something worth considering.

Since shipping containers are well-known for being eco-friendly, decorating the inside to fit this theme is a fun idea. But a shipping container really lends itself to any kind of theme. Within a small space, you can go wild with colors and little additions. A green-themed house could be filled with potted plants, stone backwashes, and bamboo furniture. With dark reds and neon blues, you could make it look like the set of the movie *Blade Runner*. Someone who wants to live in the past could furnish it using aesthetics that resemble the Baroque era so that inside their shipping container home is a little sealed-off piece of history.

That is what it all comes back to: a shipping container home is an outlet for your creativity, and there is no limit to the ideas you can pursue.

Planning Time

The first step to turning any dream into a reality is to plan it out. So, when you decide to build a shipping container home, first you'll need to get out a pen and some paper. Check out the financials, look at the space you'll need, and get the outer structure down on paper. What's the minimum budget you can manage, and what will that pay for? What would you like to include if you could? At what part of the process would you know if changes are a possibility?

Here are a few pointers to make sure your planning process is on track:

What do you actually need?

Is this a dwelling for just one person? A couple? A family? Think about how many bedrooms you'll need. Working from there, think about the bathrooms. Next, the floor space is an issue. You're dealing with a narrow container, so you'll have to be clever about keeping it open and avoiding overcrowding. Don't forget about the storage space. We all have stuff that we need to put somewhere. Your storage space is more important than you might realize. Check how much space it takes up in your current home.

Where are you going to build the home?

First, think about the country you live in. Wherever you are, there are likely to be zoning requirements. After those have been factored into your plans, then it's time to explore the site itself.

This question influences a number of other considerations, including zoning requirements for your intended location, soil type and foundation, as well as utility planning. Look into the soil and its load-bearing capacity. You might need to consult a geotechnical engineer for this. The results will let you know how deep you have to dig down and backfill for your foundation and give you some solid strategies for setting up the foundation and utilities. The site placement will shape a lot of other construction factors as well.

What do you want to spend?

In most cases, the budget is going to determine the extent of the build. If you are one of those people who doesn't have to worry about the budget, more power to you. However, most of us are looking for the best value. When you are planning your home, consider whether you're getting a new, used, or one-time-use container. Also, how many containers? Think about transportation and conversion costs, contractor scheduling (if and when you need it), and the cost of the land. This has to be factored in. Make sure to consider the skills and materials required for dressing out the interior. You're going to need a roof for most builds too, so make sure that this finds its way into the budget list.

Ok, so now you must choose whether to go prefab and have it all done for you, or if you're going to build the kit when it arrives. Or if you've got the skills, time, and money, you might choose to do the entire thing yourself. Prefab is going to be the most expensive option of the bunch, especially if you choose to have all the work done for you. It's a bit cheaper with the kits, but the real money saver is to build it yourself. You'll need to cut the windows and doors, frame them, set up the foundation, and the deck if you want one. If you can do that, then you're well on your way! Don't forget about utilities. You may need to bring someone in to do that part; however, it'll be well worth the expense. Finally, it's always a good idea to include an extra 10% in the budget all around. This will make sure you're covered if any issues arise.

When do you want to move in?

Planning is important. You have to take into account delivery of the container, any rental equipment, and deals with contractors. Make sure to speed up your timetable relative to typical builds, as the shipping container cuts out a large portion of the time and work needed. You can have your home up in no time, but you have to be ready for the steps as they come.

Is your plan realistic?

If you're going prefab, this is pretty much a no-brainer. You know what you're paying and when it can be put up. They'll take care of contracting and assembly for you. However, when we plan to do the work ourselves, we've got to look into it. Have you ever managed a build before? Do you feel confident doing it for a home that will be your home for the foreseeable future? You'll need to make sure you've got all the skills, materials, financial resources, planning permission, and other necessities required for building construction.

Permits and Zoning Laws

Before getting into some of the more complicated aspects of shipping container home construction, let's look into the building codes for different countries. Each country has its own deal regarding regulations and building zone requirements. You'll have to factor in how many people are already housed within the lot and how high you are allowed to build. It'll pay off in spades to be familiar with the zoning requirements for your region. Let's look into some of the countries in which you are most likely to build a home and what you'll have to do to build in each of them:

United Kingdom—If you want to build in the UK, the first step is to get permission from the council. Check with the local planning authorities to find out what they have to say about planning and design. It's no good to build your structure just to have the council later tell you that you have to make major changes. The list of documents provided below will give you a head start. From there, the council will be able to let you know if they need any more information.

Australia—Before getting going with a build in Australia, first check out state requirements. Plan that into your checklist, and then move forward with the local council. Make sure that your build complies with both state and council regulations. You'll be able to get paperwork from them that legitimizes all building actions. Contact them first and you'll be set throughout planning and development.

US—The bad news is that if you're building in the US, you're going to need a building permit for most places. You can get this by going to the local public works department. They can give you a full rundown of the zone your building falls in and the requirements needed for it. Just take this into account in your design, and you'll be good to go. You can set up your home to fit your needs and the building codes at the same time.

If you're especially lucky, you'll fall outside of zoning codes. Put simply, that means you can build however you want without a building permit. If you want, you can even select a site specifically because it's outside of the zoning requirements. Remember, though, that out-of-the-way sites will have restricted access to water, telephone, and power facilities. You'll have to factor this into the equation when choosing your building site.

New Zealand—Now, this is one country that is on the mark when it comes to shipping container homes. They passed a building act in 2004 that covered every aspect of shipping home construction. You'll have to get consent for them unless it's clear that you're only using them for storage. You can also check with the territorial authority. It's not unheard of for them to exempt your home from building consent, so long as it still meets code. So, once you've got your site and design authorized by them, it should be a cinch to clear it with the local government.

General List of Documents Required

Though each council or local authority will have its own specifications and regulations, here are a few things you can expect to need. Remember that regulations may influence aspects of design, so it's wise to approach your local authority before spending valuable time and energy finalizing your design.

- Structural engineering plans and approval.

- Before and after elevations.

- Site plan.

- Fully dimensioned working drawings.

- Building regulation drawings (to scale.)

Design Time!

This is where things really start to get fun. How do you want to set up your home? Where do you want the bathrooms and bedrooms? Kitchens and living areas? It's time to get something on paper. Think about how you can make it the most efficient structure it can be without sacrificing living space or aesthetics. Plus, you can make it as tall or wide as you want. You could even begin with a single container and build onto it as time and resources become available.

The easiest way to do it is to make a single-story home with as many containers as you need placed next to one another. We'll go over the details for removing adjoining walls and connecting your containers later, but everyone's going to need a bathroom, bedroom, living room, kitchen, and pantry. You can get creative and fit them all into a single 20 ft. container, or you can expand the space you're working with and make something phenomenal. The choice is yours.

So, before you go out and buy what you think you need, have a look at some of the free online software for designing shipping container homes. Just do a Google search, and you'll find everything you need to completely design your home. If you don't want to set the plans up yourself, then you might want to hire an architect. If so, then remember to factor that cost into the budget. If you're only asking for a small space to design, an architect might not cost you all that much. However, play around with the software and see what you come up with. You may surprise yourself. You can set up the design yourself and avoid the expense of an architect altogether. Alternatively, there are a number of websites that sell pre-designed container home plans. With these there will be less room for customization, but they can be a real cost-saver if you find one you love!

Planning Checklist

- Plan out the needs for your home.

- Set your budget.

- Meet with the local planning authorities to find the specifications and required paperwork for your area.

- Obtain planning permission, if necessary.

- Design your home!

Sourcing the Containers

So, you have a design now. You know exactly what you need and what your budget is. Now it's time to source the containers. That means you're looking around and checking out prices. Most of all, it means that you'll need to know the lingo and the right questions to ask.

The first step is looking into the dimensions of the containers themselves. You can opt for either the 40 ft. or 20 ft. version. They also come in both standard and high cubes. High cubes are about a foot taller than standard, with 9 ft. 6 inches of interior height. This extra foot could be great when you're thinking about storage space, ceilings, or headroom for tall people.

Have a think about where you want to put it, availability in your local area, and the overall plans you've drawn up. It's best to purchase local, or at least close, if you want to cut out unnecessary shipping costs. Plus, the tolerances for each manufacturer are slightly different. If you want the most seamless and economical home, then try to get all of your containers from the same manufacturer.

New or Used?

When you're sourcing your container, one of the first considerations is whether you want to go for a brand new container or a used one. If you choose to go new, then you can request for the floor to be built of safer wood, without the typical pesticides and other toxins. If you pick a used container, you're going to want to inspect it. You have two options here as well. Either choose a single-use container that is unlikely to have taken much damage, or go for an out-of-service container and deal with the rust and dents that come with it.

One-trip containers are the best option to balance value and structural integrity. Plus, you won't have to worry about much rust, mold, or exposure to toxic chemicals. They are usually in better condition than those that have been delivering loads for the last decade. When you convert it into a home, this means a longer life expectancy and reduced construction time. When you're working with something solid, it doesn't take much to shape it how you need it.

At the same time, the budget may be the driving issue. If this is the case, then well-used containers might be preferable. They are often painted with lead paints and treated with pesticides, so you'll need to deal with both issues before considering them safe for habitation. However, with a new floor and a thick coat of spray foam insulation over the interior, these containers could thoroughly transform your living or working area.

When it comes time to inspect the container, here are a few things you'll want to look for:

Rust

When purchasing a used container, you can expect a certain degree of light rusting. However, if there is rusting to such an extent as the integrity of the metal is compromised, find another container. Once again, it's important to check the roof as well when doing your inspection.

Leaks

This is a big one. You don't want a leaky home, and holes that allow water also create openings for other annoyances. Make sure to check the roof of the container and inspect the walls thoroughly. Also, smell the interior of the container to see if you get a hint of mold. This is another indication of possible leaks.

Chemical Contamination

Here's where your nose will really come in handy. You want to smell for anything unusual. Containers may become exposed to pesticides or other chemical hazards when in use. Ask about the history of the container when purchasing, and do a little follow-up yourself to make sure you won't be exposing yourself or your family to chemicals.

Functional Doors and Locks

Make sure to check the doors to ensure that they swing freely, and bolt them to make sure that they fasten securely and that the seal is intact.

Wooden Flooring in Good Repair

It's natural for a container to get a bit banged up when it's in use. However, you want to inspect the wooden flooring to make sure that there are no holes or breakages. Often, the original flooring is covered with a non-permeable layer and used as is, so you may have an additional, time-consuming step in construction if you unwittingly purchase a container with broken flooring.

Where Can I Get One?

The great news is that you can buy a shipping container from pretty much anywhere. Everywhere in the world, you can find disused stocks of them. The key is to find someone reputable. Look in your area with a simple Google search, and you'll be able to find all the best deals in your neighborhood. Just look for, "buy shipping containers in…" and you'll find everything you need. Alternatively, you can look for, "shipping container dealer in…" If the dealer is reputable and the containers look good, you're set.

You know how the internet is. As soon as there is a want, there's a site. So, for all those of you wanting a shipping container, one easy resource is GreenCube Network. It's a search tool like Skyscanner that checks out all the best shipping containers, automatically factoring in price, distance, and anything else you need to consider. It'll clue you into a list of dealers that will have any kind of shipping container you want.

Here's the GreenCube Network link:

http://www.greencubenetwork.org/shipping-container-dealers_3/

If you would like an alternative or you have trouble with GreenCube, feel free to check out eBay, Gumtree, or AliBaba.

What's the Price by Size?

The details are going to vary quite a bit from one supplier to another. Plus, you'll have to look into the condition of the container. As of 2016, these were some pretty good estimates of what you'd be likely to pay for a shipping container:

Dimensions	New	New	New	Used	Used	Used
	U.S. (USD)	Australia (AUD)	U.K. (GBP)	U.S.	Australia	U.K.
20 ft. Standard	$3500	$4000	£2150	$2300	$2900	£1500
20 ft. High Cube	$3500	$4250	£2300	$2400	$3000	£1600
40 ft. Standard	$5900	$7400	£3800	$3000	$3800	£2000
40 ft. High Cube	$6000	$7700	£3900	$3100	$4000	£2100

Pro Tip: You go local if you want to drop the shipping costs as much as possible and if you want to be able to see the goods before they're delivered. Check the container out in person, and you're much more likely to end up with something that you actually want. Plus, by keeping it local, you're stimulating the economy in the town around you rather than halfway across the world. Just remember to make the delivery site as close as possible to the foundation.

Remember to get the site prepared before shipping the container. If you've got the foundation in place, the next few steps flow like butter.

Container Purchasing Checklist

- Determine your budget for containers.

- Make any design adjustments necessary, factoring in the price of available containers.

- Decide on new, used, or one-time use containers.

- Source the containers from a reliable local supplier.

- If possible, inspect the container before purchase.

Chapter Four: How to Purchase Shipping Containers

The quality of your house and the success of the build will depend on the type of shipping container that you purchase, the quality of the container, the age of the container, and the dimensions of the container.

Shipping containers come in many different sizes and dimensions. When converting a container into a residence, you will quickly discover that there are advantages to each size. You will find that the standard 20-foot cube makes a great studio-style home while the 40-foot-high cube offers additional vertical space. The size or sizes that you will require will greatly depend on your build, your budget, and the location's zoning requirements. Your contractor and your architect, if you are working with either, will undoubtedly have their own opinions and suggestions as to what type of containers they would prefer. While there are many sizes of shipping containers available, these are the sizes and dimension used most often for home construction:

Standard 20 foot

- 19'10 ½ x 8' x 8'6

- 6.06m x 2.44m x 2.59m

Standard 40 foot

- 40' x 8' x 8'6

- 12.19m x 2.44m x 8.9m

High cube 20 foot

- 19'10 ½ x 8' x 9'6

- 6.06m x 2.44m x 2.90m

High cube 40 foot

- 40' x 8' x 9'6

- 12.19m x 2.44m x 9.6m

The internal dimensions may have slight variations, usually of about 5-6 inches in length, approximately 2 inches in width, and can vary approximately 6 inches in height. Not only is the size a factor in choosing the best, most durable shipping container for your build, but also the container type. There are numerous varieties of shipping containers manufactured for different purposes, and a few types lend themselves to conversion into homes. Of all the shipping containers available, dry freight containers are considered to be among the best suited for construction. They may also be referred to as cube containers; they are enclosed on all sides and open on one end only. You will also want to look for shipping containers that are constructed of Cor-Ten Steel. This type of steel is made to withstand all weather conditions and to be resistant to rust.

Once you have located a source for your shipping containers, you will want to inspect them thoroughly (if possible) before purchasing them for residential construction purposes. If you're purchasing a used container, inspection is highly recommended. You will want to ensure that the condition of the shipping container is good and sound. New containers or containers used for just one trip will cost a little more but will be in the best condition overall. Well used containers will be inexpensive, but may be in less habitable condition.

When inspecting a potential shipping container, you will want to pay close attention to the following:

1.   **Rust**—As stated above, condition is everything. Examine potential containers thoroughly for any signs of damage or rust. Keep in mind that few dings may give it character, but many will leave your home looking damaged and unattractive. Pay attention to rust. You will not want to purchase a container that

has a lot of rust. Rust is common in older, more used containers, and will require a lot of hard work to combat and may have even weakened the metal.

2. **Leaks**—Thoroughly inspect the container for leaks. Containers are designed to be waterproof, so there should be no leaks. If you spot any, be aware that the metal may have weakened in the area where the leak originated.

3. **Mold**—Mold and mildew can be tell-tale signs of both leaks and rust damage. You may want to reconsider any container that reeks of mold or even has the faintest hint of it.

4. **Pesticides and chemicals**—Be diligent about searching for any and all traces of pesticides, chemicals, or dangerous toxins. This is especially important if you are considering purchasing a used container.

5. **The roof and exterior**—Inspect the roof from the outside and the interior. You may notice leaks, rust, or corrosion from outside the container better and faster than you would have from just inspecting the insides.

Making the Decision

First, make sure you have decided that this is honestly something you want to spend time and money on. Just like building a normal home, this is not a decision that should be made at the drop of a hat. Remember the risks that come with the property. Only when you feel that this is the right decision for you to make, continue on with the next step. What comes next is the planning phase, and several logistical decisions need to be made before you start calling around.

Where Will You Put It?

Once you have gone through with your purchase, you will need a place to put your new home. Make sure that whatever property you are building on, it is legal to do so on, and that you will be able to connect to the city's plumbing. Within a city, you will have to obtain a building permit. If you live in an area where shipping container homes are a little more common, this should be a bit easier. But if the city has never had to deal with it before, it could take time. Reports have come in that it has taken up to two years for buyers to get their building permit through in certain areas. Several U.S. citizens have chosen instead to build outside of the city's zoning code, therefore bypassing the need for a building permit. Whatever way you choose to do it, so long as you know exactly where the shipping container will go, and that you have the permission to do so, you are in the clear to move on.

Pick a Type

What size would you like your house to be? Make sure this choice is made based on your own comfort level, as well as the size of land you plan to build it on. The standard sizes for all intermodal freight containers, as discussed, are either 20ft or 40ft. They can be found in smaller cuts, the smallest being 6ft, but keep in mind that the two heights listed are what containers are built in. "Standard Height" refers to the usual 8ft 6 inches. "High Cube" refers to 9ft 6 inches in height. If you have plans for a certain size, only to purchase the wrong one, you will have to rearrange your interior plans. Knowing what size you want for your doors and windows, and how many you want, is central to the consideration of what size container you want to purchase.

Grades

There are three grades that sellers use for description, referring to the quality of the container:

A-Grade refers to a fresh, almost new container. These are the ones that likely only made one trip, and have clean paint jobs and minimal denting. If you don't want to put a lot of work into fixing and updating the container, this is the grade for you.

B-Grade will have dents and rust. They are a middle-ground option, not quite fresh and new, but not completely wrecked either.

C-Grade refers to the lowest quality, meaning they will have dents, holes, and rusting. These require the most work but are the cheapest options on the market. What it comes down to is this: how much work do you want to put into it? If you only want to use the container as a base and you plan to build around it with other materials, it might be worth buying the cheaper option.

The Search

Now that you have the size and grade in mind, you can begin your search online. You can do this easily by searching for shipping containers for sale in your area. It can be anywhere from Craigslist to a simple Google search. This will be easier if you live near a coast or a port city, but that doesn't mean it is impossible if you are landlocked. After all, the fad is growing, and more shipping containers are being moved out every day. While searching, put the parameters for size and grade in. Find every available option in your area before making any calls. If it helps, you can write them down, or make a spreadsheet to compare options. Be sure to list them in order of desirability, so in case your first choice does not pan out, you can move on to your second, then third, and so forth. Once you have your choices in order, contact the seller. Like any sale, begin with a question, and be sure to specify the size and grade in the query. For example: "I saw the ad for the 20ft, A-Grade, standard height shipping container. Is it still available?" Wrangle any pictures and extra information from the seller that you can before agreeing on a meeting.

Inspection

When you first see the shipping container, it is like seeing any other house on the market. Make sure you do a full inspection. This goes for the outside and the interior. Is it up to the grade you asked? Are there any flaws that will cost you extra to fix? When inside, close the doors and check for light sources to identify any small holes. Also, if they don't seal completely, there is something wrong with the lining, and it needs to be included in the renovation. Don't let anything slip past you. Whatever flaws you find lead into the next point.

Negotiations

It is well known in the world of property investment that you never settle for the set price. Give it a haggle. There are always new containers being taken off ships, so sellers like to get things off their hands as quickly as possible. Use that to your advantage and come to an agreement that suits you both.

Delivery

If you can, have the company you bought the shipping container from deliver it to you. Most should do this already, but if it is not stated clearly in the contract, have it added in. If you are buying from an independent seller, they may be able to arrange delivery, but it won't always be possible. In that case, it will be up to you to arrange delivery from a professional delivery company. Don't get caught up in the idea that you can move it yourself, for it is very unlikely that your vehicle was made for the transport of shipping containers.

Chapter Five: Converting Your Container

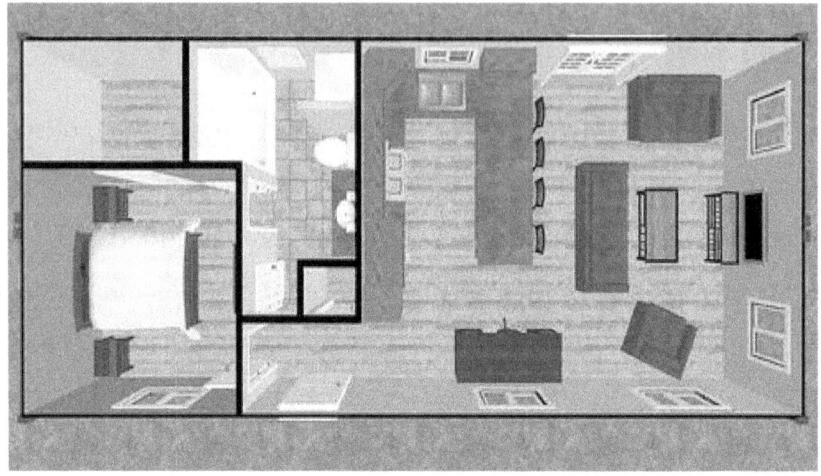

Container conversion is when things really start to get fun. To convert your container, you'll need to get out the plasma torch or cutting wheel and make the openings for your doors, windows, and adjoining walls. You may need to check with an engineer to find out what reinforcement is necessary. This will also let you know which walls need to be removed in the conversion process. The example above is a simple plan made from two 40 ft. containers. The wall has been removed from the central portion of the house to form a large living space. You can also see where you'll have to cut out windows and doors. One cool thing about joining containers like this is that you can hardly tell where one container ends and the other begins if you do it right.

Opening Up Adjoining Containers

When most people think of metal, they think of something that has to be accepted as is. However, when you start to work with metal, the perspective starts to shift a bit. When you're cutting your doors, windows, and opening up containers, you start to see the benefit of working with a material that can be cut away wherever you want with as clean a line as you can manage. It can be shaped and welded into anything you'd like.

The first step in converting your containers is to remove the walls of adjacent containers where necessary. This will help to convert two separate containers into a larger connected space. You can skip this step if you're working with a single-container build. However, now is the time to consider how you want to deal with the pre-existing door. You may wish to incorporate them in the design or weld them entirely shut. You'll want to measure and mark out the walls that need removal for multi-container designs, then get going with the cutting wheel or plasma torch.

If the containers have been converted off-site, then the most challenging part will be lining them up as you need them. If you're converting on-site, then you have a bit more wiggle room. However, the containers still need to be set flush with one another. Don't forget to line the meeting faces with spray foam insulation if possible. Also, the containers should be connected with bolts, clamps, or welds before cutting the adjacent walls. After the walls have been cut, you'll want to weld steel plates in the gaps between the openings if you really want it to be secure. In a pinch, a combination of spray foam insulation and vinyl will do the trick, but if you're putting all this energy into it, you might as well not skimp on an important detail. So, spray your insulation, weld the plates, and finish the connecting pieces between the containers. In short, do all you can to increase the life and safety of the container.

If your new home has been converted off-site, you will only need to ensure that the interior walls' cutaways line up with one another. If converting on-site, you don't have to be so concerned with this. Just cut through the walls wherever they line up. Consult your plan to determine which walls need removal. If converting off-site, you'll need to have clear plans in place and mark the containers well before placement to ensure that each container is placed in the appropriate position to allow for larger and more complex designs.

Although this has been mentioned above, it is necessary to touch once again upon connecting the floors, roofs, and walls of adjoining containers. Once pre-converted containers have been placed together, or once walls have been removed between adjoining "rooms," the floors and roofs must be connected securely. The advised method for this is welding. A 2" x ⅛" steel bar can be used to join containers by fastening it securely to both containers' steel with a stitch weld. Before working on the interior walls to make archways or other open spaces, follow the old adage: measure twice, cut once. Mark the cut area and make sure that the measurements are up to spec. Then follow the markings with a cutting disk, plasma torch, angle grinder, or other cutting tool of your choice. Exercise caution during this process, as the slabs of steel from the container walls are heavy, and the edges of the steel will be sharp after cutting.

Remember that you'll also need to weld the floors together to turn your two containers into a single, seamless unit after removing the adjoining walls. For most builds, you'll also want to weld the interior seams together. This strengthens the integrity of your home and reduces the potential for leaks and pests. Another important detail is structural reinforcement. If you are removing large sections of connecting wall, it will be necessary to use steel box beams running the width of the container to bear the load of the roof and ceiling. These should be stitch welded to the interior roofs of the containers. Check with a structural engineer to make sure your structure can handle all it requires.

Framing, Fitting Doors, and Windows

Once you've got your container walls cut, it's time to cut out the spaces for doors and windows, then frame and fit them. By now, the space should be looking more and more like a home. One of the best ways to go about this is to create cardboard templates for everything you need to cut out; mark out the areas with a permanent marker, then just cut away. Plasma torches, some cutting wheels, or any other number of power tools can work. If you have the needed supplies, you can have a lot of fun with this stage. Just remember that the edges, after they've been cut, can be pretty sharp. Also, don't forget to wear a mask when making the cuts.

After preparing the openings, or even before, you can create your window and door frames. Remember to get a level involved here. Small shifts in angle can make pretty large structural changes, especially with doors. Fit the frames into their spaces and weld the assembly to the frame of the container. If you have any gaps after the welding, you can seal them with mastic sealant to keep the outer shell of your home watertight. At this point, you should be fully equipped with open spaces between containers, welded seams connecting adjoining parts, areas for doors, windows, and frames that really make them pop.

Making the Frames

It's pretty simple here. Before you can fit and weld the frames, you've got to be able to make them. That, or you're using prefab frames designed for this purpose. Either answer is fine. However, if you're doing it yourself, then make sure to measure out the doors and windows. Once you have the measurements, cut lengths of square 50 x 50 mm galvanized steel tubing with a 2 mm thickness. Cut the ends at 45-degree angles so that they can be stitched welded together to construct the frames.

To ensure that the measurements are correct, lay the frame against the window or door to make sure it fits. If the frame is snug in the space, remove the door or window and then weld them together. Once it has been welded, you can smooth the assembly using a grinder with a flap disk. Afterward, spray the entire frame on both sides with galvanized paint. This will help to prevent corrosion.

Creating the Opening

When cutting the openings for the doors and windows, you will follow much the same process as you have for removing the interior walls. First, measure the dimensions of the desired opening and mark them out upon the container's steel wall. Next, use an angle grinder, plasma cutter, or cutting torch to carefully remove the steel and allow the cut section to drop away. Make sure to include the frame in your template, as the opening will need to be large enough to house it.

A plasma cutter will offer the cleanest lines and is preferable if you are planning to reuse the steel. However, some may not have access to one or the experience to use it properly. If this is the case, then an angle grinder is the cheapest and most DIY-friendly option. Keep in mind that it's hard to cut a really accurate and straight line with an angle grinder. It's going to take a bit of patience, but if you go slowly and surely, you'll be able to make the cuts you need. After doing the work, you'll probably want to spend some time on the edges with a flap disk to smooth everything out. Once you've got the edges cleaned up, you can move on to welding your frames to the container.

Hanging Your Doors and Windows

So, you've got your openings and your frames now. The next step is to put them together. Place the frames inside the openings, ensure they're oriented correctly, and then secure them with welds or self-tapping screws. Screws are the quicker option and likely better for those without much welding experience. However, welding is stronger and holds up better without the need for repairs. If that is your choice, then affix the frame to the container with a stitch weld.

Welded areas, screw holes, and any other exposed metal areas will be prone to rust. To prevent this, you'll want to break out the galvanized paint again and cover the exposed areas. Pay special attention to the corners of the frame, as they're one of the weak spots in this process. Grab some elastomeric sealant to plug any gaps that remain between the frame and container. Caulk is ideal for this purpose. Another option for filling gaps is mortar.

Either way will work, but once the holes have been filled, you'll need to cover the sealant, frame, and connecting area of the container with latex-based paint to prevent leakage and rust.

At this point, the conversion process is pretty much complete. If you've already installed a roof, you can move along to the floors and framing. If not, then you'll want to install a rain deflector over all your openings. An easy way to do this is to place a 2" x ⅛" steel plate a few inches above the opening and weld it into place with a stitch weld. This will keep water off the assembly and protect it further from deterioration.

Doors, Windows, and Removal of Interior Walls Checklist

- Measure, mark, and cut away adjoining walls to make larger interior spaces.

- Create the frames for your doors and windows.

- Measure and cut the openings for your doors and windows.

- Weld window and door frames into place.

- Hang windows and doors, securing them in place.

- Smooth the welds, cover with sealant, and go over exposed areas with latex paint.

Chapter Six: Decorating Your Shipping Container Home

While shipping container homes can be considered to be quite unconventional, interior design options for your home might be equally as obscure. This chapter will focus on ways that you can decorate the inside of your home in order to accentuate its overall design. Before you begin buying stuff with which to decorate your new and exciting home, it might be helpful to consider an overall theme that will contribute to the general feeling of the space as a whole. Additionally, this chapter will give you great tips on how to save space, something that every smart shipping container homeowner should strive to achieve.

Interior Design Option 1: Curtains

Many shipping container homes are highly reliant on curtains. Because of how dark a container would be without windows, big and expansive ones are often a staple of well-designed homes. This being the case, curtains are almost a must for a shipping container home. The picture below is a great example of how to maximize the use of curtains. These curtains enclose both the porch and the windows inside the home simultaneously, so that both can be obscured at the same time. Oftentimes in modular home design, less is more!

Interior Design Option 2: Reflective Glass

While this option should technically be considered "exterior," reflective glass for your windows is another great option if curtains are simply not your thing. Opting for reflective glass allows you to forego the use of curtains so that you can see out even though no one can see in. Privacy is important, even if you live in a rather secluded area. Reflective glass should definitely be considered if your shipping container home is located where you have access to great views on a daily basis, or are surrounded by people eager to look inside your unique home.

Interior Design Option 3: Stacking Rooms

Another way to design the tight space on the inside of your container home is to stack rooms or beds. In the picture above, you can see that the sleeping area is above the living room or television watching area. Attached to the base of the living room area is a rod with a thick dark curtain on it so that the bed can be isolated from the living room and surrounding kitchen area. Of course, it might be a bit hard to sleep if someone is watching television as you're getting ready to go to bed, but when you choose to live in a container home, the reality is that noise pollution may sometimes contaminate the space.

Interior Design Option 4: Fold-Out Table

A fold-out table is a fabulous way to design a kitchen area in a container home because it gives the home greater utility and versatility. It also allows more square footage to exist in the house when dinner isn't being served. A container home can always use more space, and a fold-out table provides just that. Additionally, in the photo below, the table is attached to a dresser of sorts. The china on the dresser along with books and a speaker suggest that this shelving unit is used for both the bedroom and the eatery. This type of shelving unit, with openings on either end of it, also serves to provide more space to the entire area of the home.

Lastly, take note of the drawers beneath the bed. On top of the drawers is a bench that can be used as a place to sit while eating. While you would still need to use collapsible chairs at the opposite end of the table if you were dining with more than a couple of people, the multidimensional ability of this drawer/bench combination offers a simplified design tactic.

Interior Design Option 5: From Table to Framed Photo

In addition to simply folding a table and letting the legs of the table be exposed on the wall, you can opt to design or buy a collapsible table that has a photo or painting on its underside. In the example provided, the table legs are cut in a way that allows them to be used as a frame when they are folded and on the wall. This is an even more innovative way to hide your table when it's not being used. When you invite an individual into your home, this idea is sure to be one that will attract some comments.

Chapter Seven: Risks Involved with a Shipping Container Home

With all the talk of how fiscally sensible and innovative the shipping container home movement is, you may be wondering why everyone isn't doing it. There seem to be no flaws in the plan, but despite the many rewards, there are still risks that come with choosing to live in a shipping container. It is important to understand all these risks before you make your decision. Don't let this chapter scare you away. Every kind of homeowner can tell you that different risks come with different kinds of investments. A purchase of a condominium comes with a completely different set of risks than a purchase of a float home. Everything comes with ups and downs, and that's simply a part of owning a home. What you need to know is how to identify the particular set of risks that come with your chosen investment, and figure out whether you can deal with them.

The most important thing to remember is this: not every challenge is something you can overcome on your own. You cannot just venture out to purchase a shipping container and expect that you alone will be able to turn it into a healthy, safe, and comfortable space. Unless you already do these sorts of things for a living, it will require a coordinated effort between groups of professionals. Make sure you know and trust the people you choose to help you in this endeavor, as with any kind of housing, one misstep can cause a lifetime of problems to follow.

Steel

As previously stated, the intermodal freight containers used in this type of housing are made of steel. On its own, steel is not a proper material used for habitable buildings. While it is strong and durable, it conducts heat. During warm weather, any open metal surfaces will be hot to the touch, sometimes to the point of burning. The air inside can also become dangerously heated if not properly ventilated or cooled. Likewise, in cold weather, all heat is conducted out of the container. It can be as cold inside the space as it is outside. For these reasons, it is imperative that your shipping container home is properly insulated. This is not something the cost can be skimped on, nor something you only want to do halfway. Another problem steel faces, is the tendency to rust. In high temperatures, the air inside the container will humidify, akin to the bathroom after a hot shower or a steam room at the local gym. If that moisture is allowed to accumulate on any open steel surface, it will rust over time. This, too, can be avoided by properly insulating your container. A sealant also should be used to increase longevity.

Damage

Because shipping containers have been transported across oceans, there is a good chance they will have sustained some damage on the voyage. The last thing you want is to purchase a container only to have it fall apart during the renovation. There could be either external or internal damage, and sometimes both. Any spot on the container that has been scraped or broken through needs to be sufficiently patched up. Upon inspection, containers may also be condemned or otherwise deemed unsafe for use as homes.

Health Hazards

Intermodal freight containers were obviously not designed with human habitation in mind. For that matter, they were not designed for any sort of habitation. The insides are full of insecticides and other poisons meant to prevent the containers from becoming the home of any wayward pests. Measures need to be taken to prevent your new house from being toxic. The insides should be abrasively blasted to get rid of any toxins, and then repainted with a non-hazardous paint. This includes the floors where some of the most dangerous toxins can gather. New flooring will also have to be installed. Remember, this is on top of the sealant and insulation you need in the inside walls. If this feels like a lot to go through, keep in mind that it is for your own health. Plenty of this kind of safety preparation goes into the building of regular houses and apartment complexes too, we just don't realize it because we are not involved in the process like we are here.

Now, sometimes these problems can be fixed before buying. Plenty of sellers won't even put a container on the market unless it is 100% safe for use. Still, even if you trust them completely, have it looked at by a professional. Some things can be missed. Even if it is deemed completely ready for habitation, there are other things you need to consider.

When you go in for a shipping container, it won't have any windows, proper doors, heating, plumbing, air conditioning, electricity, or any basic amenities that seem like a given when shopping for homes. Having your shipping container fitted with these is going to cost you, and will need to factor these into your budget during the planning phase. You also need to consider how much of this renovation you are planning to do yourself. If you are not an experienced plumber, electrician, or have never worked construction before, you are going to have a hard time fitting your container. And if you don't have the basic amenities, you have no foundation to go on and make all your fancy interior designs. So, hiring a contractor to direct the renovation for you will also have to be a part of your budget. When it comes down to it, the risks are not insurmountable, it just means that you need to do a great deal of planning and preparation. As long as you are aware of all the above things that can cut into the price, and budget for them accordingly, it will not impede your progress.

So, before making the decision, take some time to sit down and think it over. Have a conversation with friends or family, people with unbiased opinions that you can trust to bounce ideas off of. Really make sure that you've weighed all your options. Investing in a shipping container home is no different than investing in any other kind. As long as you've done the preparations, thought it through completely, and have a team of people behind you to help along the way, you're on the road to success.

Chapter Eight: Insulation

As you are by now aware, your shipping container home is created out of a big metal box. Metal is an excellent conductor. It absorbs temperature easily, and these temperatures will come into your container if you're not careful. Without insulation, you'll be living inside an oven for half the year, and a freezer for the other half. This means either challenging living conditions or very high heating and cooling costs. On top of issues with heat, without insulation you'll also have to deal with condensation. Condensation happens whenever one side of a surface is colder than another. Water vapor on the warmer side will precipitate out of the air to coat the surface. This can lead to rust or leaks and, if left for a while, can cause mold as well. These complications will either further compromise the structure of the container or pose a health hazard to your family.

Insulation Options

If you are going to insulate, how should you go about it? Well, just like any other step of the way, you've got some options. The first thing to consider is this: internal, external, or both? Since this is such a weak point for shipping container homes, it's recommended to insulate both the inside and outside surfaces, but it's really up to you. If you do live in a cold climate, exterior insulation is definitely a must. It'll keep heat loss down between the container and the surrounding cold air. The more extreme your climate, the better it is to use a combination of internal and external insulation.

External Insulation

Think about the physics here. Without external insulation, your container will still heat up. This heat will surround the space and seep in past the internal insulation as much as it's able to. And we're talking about a lot of heat here. In colder times, the heat goes the other way, out of the container from the warmer interior. So, external insulation will keep the container cooler in the summer and warmer in the winter. It'll cut your heating and cooling costs dramatically and help to keep your home comfortable. In addition to helping out with heat considerations, insulation can also be a great way to touch up the exterior of your container and provide a different finish. You can fill in the voids of the corrugated walls with insulation if you like, though this could be expensive. After the walls have been lined with spray foam insulation, they'll be ready for proper paint or cladding.

However, if you are just insulating the exterior, you'll save yourself another inch or so of floor and ceiling space. It's especially important to insulate the underside of the container. The best time to do this, for easiest and fastest process, is when placing the container. If you are unable to do this, however, it's best to install insulation beneath the flooring. If you had planned to leave the interior walls of the container unmodified, external insulation is ideal. It will let you preserve every available inch of floor space. You'll also want to line the roof of the container with insulation. It's fairly easy to do this underneath a new roof. After placing the roof beams, you can lay rolls of insulation out between the beams. This isn't extremely necessary if you have already covered the roof with spray foam. At the same time, it can shave thousands off of your heating and cooling costs each year. If you choose to insulate the roof and leave the ceiling of the container bare, then you will be left with a bit more headroom. However, if you're already planning to install a ceiling, a layer of insulation inside won't cost you any extra height.

Internal Insulation

Internal insulation isn't absolutely necessary, but it is a really great addition. If you plan to panel the walls and install a ceiling, then you lose no space on account of the insulation. Just as a reminder, uninsulated ceilings will collect condensation when cooking and whenever it's hotter inside than outside. Use spray foam insulation on the interior of your container, then you can cover up any scratches, dents, or marks that might be on the surface of the container. It also gives you a great surface to paint on. This may not be the best option in colder climates, but it does hold a certain aesthetic appeal if you can manage it. When thinking about internal insulation, the biggest factor to take into account is that it's going to take up space. Space is a limiting factor with shipping container construction, so you'll want to keep this in mind during the planning stage. Another option is to use internal insulation in some places and external in others. You can also double up where you like.

Insulation Placement

The key here is to insulate all faces of the container. You've got the bottom, the top, the two sides, and the two ends. External insulation is a must for the bottom of the container and highly recommended for the roof. The roof is actually an easy part of the process. After placing your container, you can just pop up top and spray foam or lay the insulation as you're constructing the roof. It helps to back this up with insulation placed against the ceiling, but you've got ample space to insulate the top during roof construction, while space can be limited later.

When you're dealing with the interior walls, once again, it depends on whether you're using panels, rolls, or spray foam. Spray foam insulation can be applied before any other work on the interior. If you are using a blanket or panel, it can be placed right between the battens. When installing a blanket or panel installation on the ceiling, you can place it between the joists.

When installing insulation for the floor of the container, line the inner floor before installing the subfloor.

Types of Insulation

As you may have gathered from the passages above, you have a few options when it comes to insulation: spray foam, insulation panels, and blankets or rolls. Each option has certain advantages and disadvantages, so we'll take a closer look at each.

Blanket or Roll Insulation

Roll or blanket insulation is the cheapest of the three options. The most common style of blanket insulation is mineral, also commonly known as "rock wool." Installation requires the construction of stud walls, as the rock wool rolls are placed between the battens and rolled down into place. Once the stud walls have been constructed, it's quick and easy to place. The installation is simple, but it should be remembered that blanket insulation is made of fiberglass and should be handled carefully. You'll want gloves and masks, and you may want to cover your skin as well. When compared to spray foam, installing blanket or panel insulation is far cleaner, but it takes a bit more time and effort. You will need to have a stud wall framed prior to installation. After the wall has been framed, the same steps are followed for both blankets and panels.

Essentially, all you need to do is place the panels or blankets in the gaps between the studs. Try to plan the width of battens and blankets or panels so you can insulate the space without cutting. This is not only more efficient but also reduces construction time. If you're using blanket insulation, you'll want to place the foil side against the wall of the container.

Spray foam insulation is the easiest way to go about insulating the bottom and top of the container. However, if you want to use roll or panel insulation on the top or bottom, then you'll need to batten out the space first. You can use 2" x 4" beams across the width of the bottom or top. Space them at about 8" or 200 mm between the centers of each. Place the rock wool between the battens just as you would do it for the interior of the building. You can combine methods with roof and foundation as well, placing insulation and then spraying an inch of foam over it to create a seal.

Tip: Some types of blanket insulation use formaldehyde as a binder. To reduce the hazardous chemicals in your home, look for formaldehyde-free blanket insulation. This has the same insulating properties without the harsh chemicals.

Panel Insulation

If you're looking for the absolute minimum hassle for construction and don't mind paying a bit more for it, then panels are the way to go. It goes up quickly, and you won't have to worry about fiberglass particles. Insulating panels are relatively thin panels with high insulating value. They can be bought in predefined sizes and placed between studs, so the installation process is almost the same as blanket insulation. However, they're thinner, and they'll leave you more space to work with. Unless you're going for the absolute cheapest option, ease of installation and reduced thickness make panel insulation worth the few extra bucks. Panel insulation can also be used for the underside of the container, though just as with blanket insulation, the foundation will need to be battened out to affix the panels.

Spray Foam Insulation

Spray foam is probably the most expensive option. It's also messy, and it requires a bit of expertise to get in place right. Because of the mess factor, you'll want to cover and tape everything that you don't want covered in spray foam. This includes doors and windows as well as pipes, utility cables, and electric sockets. A thin layer of plastic sheeting will do the trick. Cut it to size, and then fit in place with masking tape. Cables, pipes, and electric sockets can be wrapped in tape before beginning the process. You may also want to place a plastic sheet on the floor of the container to prevent overspray and time-consuming cleanup later.

Spray foam insulation can be sprayed directly onto the walls of the container, meaning that you will save time in creating battens if they aren't necessary for other purposes (like holding up paneling for interior walls.) It will take the least time of all your installations and do the best job at insulating the container. The chief upside is that you get a seamless, airtight barrier, and the highest resistance to heat flow per thickness you can get. Another advantage it has over blanket and panel insulation is that it can easily fill uneven surfaces and gaps, whereas blanket and panel insulation might have to be cut down to fill odd spaces.

Though it isn't necessary to frame the inner surface of exterior walls if insulating with spray foam, you may still choose to do so. This will allow you to place plasterboard or panels over the insulation. Plasterboard will offer a smooth surface that can then be painted, while panels offer their own unique aesthetic value. If you have chosen to go this route, simply spray foam insulation between the battens, just as you would have placed blankets or panels. If you choose not to frame the external-facing walls, then you may choose to use different nozzles when applying the spray foam. This will offer a variety of textures to the wall, ranging from smooth to pebbled.

With spray foam insulation, you will need a minimum of two inches of foam thickness on the walls. You have some options here. You can spray the entire two inches on one side of the interior or the exterior of the wall, or you can instead divide it, placing one inch on the inside and one inch on the outside. If your design involves joining two or more containers together, make sure to insulate the bolts joining the walls and the welds between adjoining floors. Place a layer of spray foam over the flat metal bars which were welded between adjoining walls, as well as over and around the bolts placed between containers.

There are a number of choices on the market when it comes to spray foam. What you're looking for is closed-cell polyurethane foam. Closed-cell spray foam is resistant to both water and vapor. It can be used externally or internally, while open-cell spray foam should only be used internally in areas which will not be subject to dampness. Closed-cell polyurethane foam also has a higher insulating value per applied thickness. When space is a premium, every inch counts. Regardless of the type of insulation you choose, remember to use the proper PPE or personal protective equipment. This includes dust masks, goggles, gloves, and protective clothing.

Final Words

Shipping container homes can provide a great solution when looking for a cheap and easy way to build a house. They are a great alternative to traditional building materials like wood and bricks. Plus, shipping containers are really easy to find, and they are relatively inexpensive. With these types of homes on the rise, there are lots of benefits that come with the territory, especially if you're going for a rustic and industrial look. The construction of building container homes is also a great way to get involved in a DIY project.

First and foremost, just because you want a luxury home doesn't mean it has to be enormous. Therefore, a nicely sized and functional home can be made out of a very limited number of these shipping containers. Even one can sometimes be appropriate. If you want to build a house from shipping containers with more living space, all you need to do is add more! With enough time and planning, any house made this way can look as good (if not better!) as those constructed with traditional methods. But the amount of money you will save overall will be substantial!

The idea is to turn these rectangular boxes into viable dwellings. The advantages are that they are highly durable and, in terms of rigidity and strength, exceed all construction requirements. They can withstand hurricane-force winds and, when put underground, are excellent tornado shelters. The biggest challenge most people face is getting the plans past the department of scheduling. However, a new uniform building code for shipping container homes is starting to work its way through the industry, so passing may be simpler by the time you get around to it!

I hope you've enjoyed learning about this new and exciting trend in the world of building and design. You should now have a good understanding of what's involved in building one of these unique homes, as well as the pros and cons of doing so. If you choose to pursue this type of housing, know that you are making a fantastic choice. I wish you the best of luck!

References

Alex W., Tristan R., Nadav M.,(July, 2016) INSULATION RECOMMENDATIONS A Quick Guide to Cost, Health, and Environmental Considerations. (n.d.).

Abrasheva, G., Senk, D., & Häußling, R. (2012). Shipping containers for a sustainable habitat perspective. Metallurgical Research & Technology, 109(5), 381-389.

Balogun, L. (2018). Shipping Container as an Alternative Housing Solution: Case Study Lagos, Nigeria.

Blanford, M., & Bender, S. (2020). Upcycling Shipping Containers for Houses. Cityscape, 22(2), 95-100.

Brandt, K. A. (2011). Plugging In: Reinterpreting the traditional housing archetype within a community using shipping containers (Doctoral dissertation, University of North Carolina at Greensboro).

Brodaski, M., Campanelli, R., & Zabinsk, K. (2010). Shipping container emergency shelters. Worcester Polytechnic Institute: Bachelor Project.

Caldwell, C., & Hänninen, M. (2021). Research and development on shipping container homes: dedicated to the Finnish market.

Container Homes - Pros, Cons & Cost Comparison. (2018, November 29). Rise.

Day, R. (1976). All about Decorating Your Home. Hamlyn.

DECORATING, Y. H., & De Reineck, M. The selection and arrangement of furnishings for the modern home. A guide to color harmony and its application to planning a room. The treatment of walls, floors and draperies. A discussion of the characteristics of period furniture. Contemporary trends and practices. Illustrated with many photographs and drawings.

Eiseman, L., & Hickey, R. (1998). Colors for your every mood: Discover your true decorating colors. Capital Books.

Forrest, A. (2015). Living in a steel box: Are shipping containers really the future of housing. The Guardian, 9.

Grębowski, K., & Kałdunek, D. (2017, October). Using container structures in architecture and urban design. In IOP Conference Series: Materials Science and Engineering (Vol. 245, No. 4, p. 042087). IOP Publishing.

Home, I. C. (2020, March 1). Electrical Wiring of Shipping Container Home. IContainerHome.Com. https://icontainerhome.com/electrical-wiring-of-shipping-container-home/

Hunt, K. (2021). The Shipping Container Homes Book: A Shipping Container House Plans to Building an Environmentally Friendly Home, Plus Tips, and Design Ideas to Get You Started. Kenelm Hunt.

Ishan, J. R. P., De Silva, N., & Withanage, K. T. (2019). Use of shipping container housing concept as a low cost housing solution for resettlement projects in urban areas.

Islam, H., Zhang, G., Setunge, S., & Bhuiyan, M. A. (2016). Life cycle assessment of shipping container home: A sustainable construction. Energy and Buildings, 128, 673-685.

John, O. U. (2020). Study Of Shipping Container Housing As An Alternative To Sandcrete Block And Reinforced Concrete In Lagos (Doctoral dissertation, Department of Architecture, College of Environmental Sciences, Bells University of Technology).

Ling, M. (2021). Container housing: Formal informality and deterritorialised home-making amid bulldozer urbanism in Shanghai. Urban Studies, 58(6), 1141-1157.

Lyons, G. H. (2008). Ten Common Home Decorating Mistakes and How to Avoid Them. Blue Sage Press.

McMillan, K. K., & McMillan, P. H. (2011). Home decorating for dummies (Vol. 178). John Wiley & Sons.

Menesatti, P., Canali, E., Sperandio, G., Burchi, G., Devlin, G., & Costa, C. (2012). Cost and waste comparison of reusable and disposable shipping containers for cut flowers. Packaging Technology and Science, 25(4), 203-215.

Morris, T. (2015). Decorating with the five elements of Feng Shui. Llewellyn Worldwide.

Oloto, E., & Adebayo, A. K. (2015). Building with shipping containers:

A sustainable approach to solving housing shortages in Lagos metropolis. Department of Architecture, University of Lagos.

Palmisano, J. (2014). Salvage Secrets Design & Decor: Transform Your Home with Reclaimed Materials: Transform Your Home with Reclaimed Materials. WW Norton & Company.

Patil, L. D., Ali, M. I., Abdallah, H. A., & Sarode, G. C. (2021). Rapid Construction of House Using Shipping Container and GFRG Panels. International Journal of Research in Engineering, Science and Management, 4(6), 241-244.

Radwan, A. H. (2015). Containers Architecture: Reusing Shipping Containers in Making Creative Architectural Spaces. International Journal of Scientific & Engineering Research, 6(11), 1562-1577.

serrajr. (2019, June 25). 5 Reasons to Buy a Container Home. ECONTAINERS. https://www.econtainersmod.com/5-reasons-to-buy-a-container-home/

Shipping Container Conditions explained | WWT, CW, As-is. (2019, February 28). Container XChange. https://container-xchange.com/blog/container-conditions-and-grading-explained/

Shipping Container Homes: A 2019 Guide to Buying & Building Container Houses. (2019, July 2).

Shipping Container Zoning, Permits, and Building Codes. (2019, August 27). Discover Containers.

https://www.discovercontainers.com/shipping-container-zoning-permits-and-building-codes-which-states-allow-them/

Smith, J. D. (2005). Shipping containers as building components. University of Brighton, Brighton.

Taleb, H., Elsebaei, M., & El-Attar, M. (2019). Enhancing the sustainability of shipping container homes in a hot arid region: A case study of Aswan in Egypt. Architectural Engineering and Design Management, 15(6), 459-474.

Tan, C. S., & Ling, P. C. (2018). Shipping Container as shelter provision solution for post-disaster reconstruction. In E3S web of conferences (Vol. 65, p. 08007). EDP Sciences.

Tomrley, C. G. (1940). Furnishing Your Home: A Practical Guide to Inexpensive Furnishing and Decorating. G. Allen & Unwin.

Ward, L. (1999). Use what You Have Decorating: Transform Your Home in One Hour with Ten Simple Design Principles Using... Penguin.

Wheeler, J., & Jl, H. (1961). Decorating Your Home With the Family in Mind. The Iowa Homemaker, 41(8), 10.

www.ingramcontent.com/pod-product-compliance
Lightning Source LLC
Chambersburg PA
CBHW071114120626
46546CB00003B/1332